To our daughter Iris and all the wonderful people who work to save our beautiful trees and wildlife. ~ R.O.

tiny seed publishing

An imprint of Starfish Bay Publishing
www.tinyseedpublishing.com

Tree-squeak the Old-growth Gum

ISBN 978-1-80036-143-0
First Published 2025
Printed in China following rigorous ethical sourcing standards.

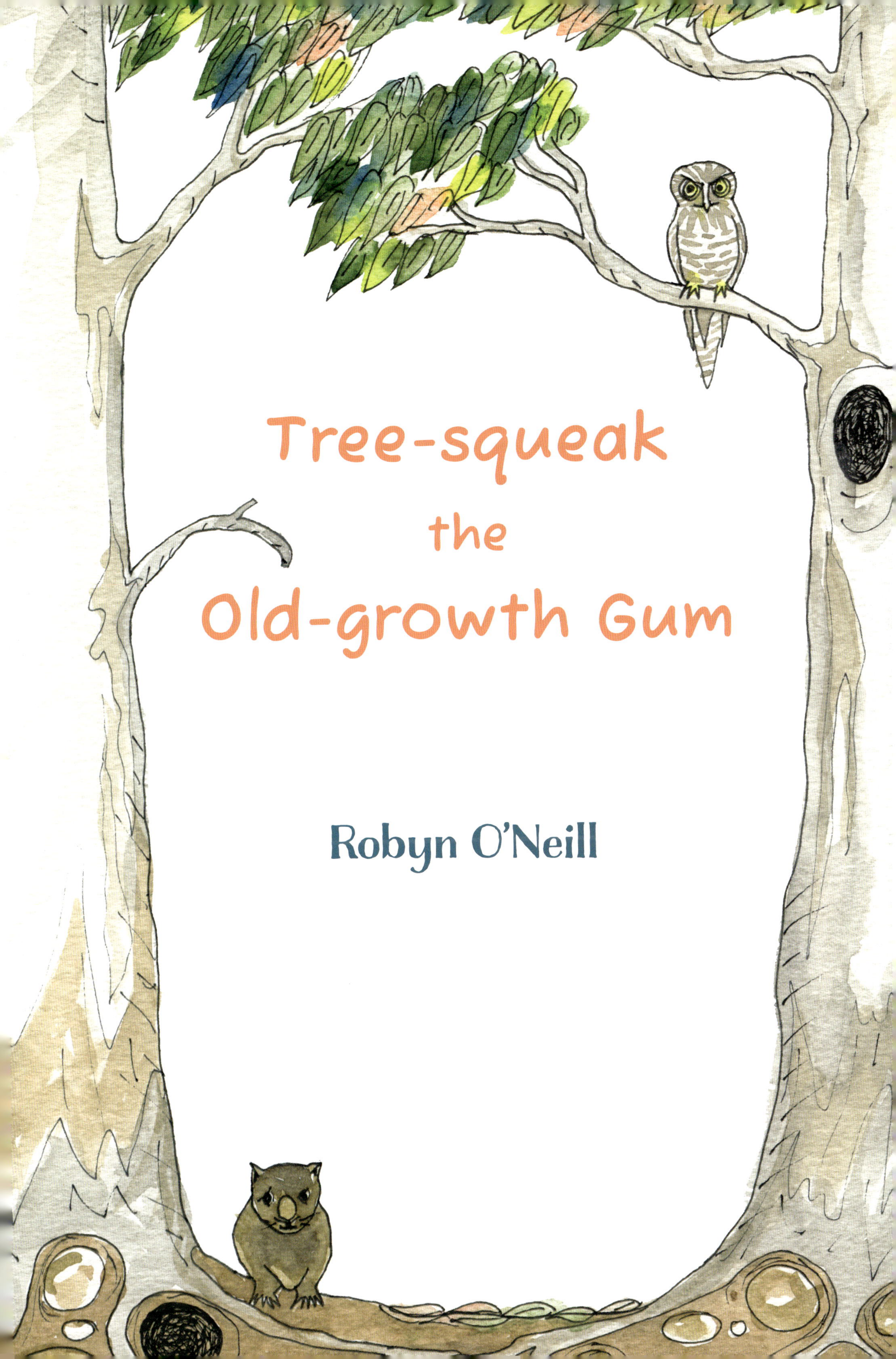

Tree-squeak the Old-growth Gum

Robyn O'Neill

Tree-squeak, the **old-growth gum**,
he's so tall he can touch the sun!
Tree-squeak, the old-growth gum,
he's older than your grandpa's mum!

Tree-squeak, the old-growth gum,
has a home for everyone,
birds, koalas, possums too.
In his branches is a ZOO!

Tree-squeak lives with plants and shrubs,
many creatures, ants and grubs.
An **ecosystem** helps all survive.
They work together to stay alive.

Tree-squeak, the old-growth gum,
on his trunk he has a chum.
She's furry, cuddly, and holds on tight
and feeds on gum leaves through the night.

Tree-squeak, the old-growth gum,
has a home for everyone.
There's a bird in a hollow you can find.
It's red and green and king of its kind.

Who's that creature
hanging upside-down?
She spreads seeds and pollen
as she flies around.

She's **nocturnal**,
so flies at night.
With her 'pup' on her back,
she's quite a sight!

At the base of the trunk,
there's a slither and hiss.
Better not give this one a kiss!
You won't die from this one's bite,
but you will get quite a fright!

Tree-squeak, the old-growth gum,
has a home away from the sun.
She digs a burrow and eats roots and grass.
She's round and furry and very FAST!

To a hollow way up high
then to its nest this bird will fly.
Very special, very rare,
the largest nightbird lives up there!

Another for whom
Tree-squeak cares,
this creature's shy
and very scared.

She nests in hollows,
where we can't see,
and glides through the night
from tree to tree.

On loping wings these birds will fly
across the grey and cloudy sky.
When these birds cry their plaintive call,
it is a sign that rain will fall.

Tree-squeak has grown new shoots and buds.
He's come back alive from fires and floods.
It's amazing how old gums regrow.
Not even a wildfire is a fatal blow.

Tree-squeak, the old-growth gum,
gives air and shade to everyone.
Climb his branches, have some fun,
but please don't fall on anyone!

Tree-squeak, he's green and brown.
Please don't come and chop him down!
Tree-squeak, the old-growth gum—
let's keep him for everyone!

Answers

Pages 6-7: Koala

Koalas live in tall open forests of eucalypts and eat the leaves of eucalypt trees. They do not drink water but get their fluids through the leaves. They are a type of **mammal** known as a **marsupial**. Female marsupials have a backward-facing pouch to carry their young, which are called 'joeys'. Koalas sleep for up to 20 hours a day. They live for up to 15 years in the wild. Did you know koalas have two thumbs?! They are listed as Vulnerable, due to deforestation, droughts, and fires.

Pages 8-9: King Parrot

King parrots are found on the east coast of Australia in eucalypt forests and rainforests, foraging for seeds and fruit. They lay their eggs in the deep hollow of a large tree. Often, the hollow is over 10 m high (30 feet) off the ground, then they fly down to their nest inside the base of the tree! Both males and females have a red belly and green back, but males have a completely red head. King parrots form lifelong mating pairs and have a lifespan of up to 25 years. A group of parrots is called a 'pandemonium' because they are so wild and noisy! Their conservation status is Least Concern.

Pages 10-11: Flying Fox

The flying fox is a megabat and the largest flying mammal in Australia. Young flying foxes are called 'pups.' They do the important job of spreading the pollen and seeds of native plants as they eat. They are **nocturnal**, so during the day, they sleep in large trees, hanging upside down in their hundreds in groups called 'camps'. Unlike most bats, they use sight and smell rather **echolocation**. They are listed as Vulnerable to extinction because of loss of **habitat**.

Pages 12-13: Diamond Python

Diamond pythons are reptiles, meaning they are cold-blooded, lay eggs, and have a spine. They grow up to 3 metres (10 feet) long. They live in bushland areas on Australia's east coast and are **nocturnal**. They kill their prey of small mammals, birds, and lizards by wrapping themselves around it and squeezing it until it suffocates. They are often found basking in or around eucalypt trees. Although they are not venomous, they can bite.
They are not listed as Endangered, but they have suffered from loss of habitat.

Pages 14-15: Wombat

Wombats are marsupial mammals, and they raise their young in a backward-facing pouch. Baby wombats are called 'puggles'. Wombats dig holes with their sharp claws and live in burrows underground in the Australian bushland. Their diet consists of native grasses and roots. They are nocturnal and can live up to 30 years old, grow up to 1 metre (3 feet) in length, and can run up to 40 km an hour (25 mph). There are three types of wombats in Australia, and the northern hairy-nosed wombat is listed as Critically Endangered. Unfortunately, many are hit by cars while crossing roads at night.

Pages 16-17: Powerful Owl

Powerful owls are the largest Australian nightbird, growing up to 65 cm (26 inches) in height, with a wingspan up to 135 cm (53 inches). They nest in vertical hollows in trees, and they mate for life. They are a powerful predator and eat smaller mammals such as possums, rats, and gliders. Their call sounds like "whoo-hoo". Powerful owls are listed as Vulnerable to extinction.

Pages 18-19: Greater Glider

These are the largest gliding marsupials in the world. They can glide up to 100 m (328 feet) at a time, and they use their long tails as a kind of rudder to change direction mid-flight. They range in colour from chocolate brown to white. They live in mum's pouch for the first three months of life, then they hitch a ride on her back for the next three months. They are completely silent as they glide. They maintain many 'dens' in tree hollows across a wide area, eating eucalypt leaves, buds, and flowers.
They are listed as Endangered from loss of habitat through logging, land-clearing, and fires.

Pages 20-21: Glossy Black Cockatoo

These are the smallest of all cockatoo species. They have a black body up to 48 cm (19 inches) long, with red and brown tail panels. Females have yellow patches on their head and tails, while the male is black with red and red-orange tail feathers. They eat the seeds of casuarina trees, which are part of the Australian forest system, and they nest in the hollows of large gum trees. They mate for life, and the male delivers food to the nesting female as she roosts. They are listed as Vulnerable.

The International Union for Conservation of Nature Red List of Threatened Species

This is a global authority on the status of the natural world and the measures needed to safeguard it. This is their measure for the threat of extinction to the world's animals.

Extinct – gone forever
Extinct in the Wild – only survives in captivity
Critically Endangered – extreme risk of extinction in the immediate future
Endangered – high risk of extinction in the near future
Vulnerable – at high risk of extinction in the medium term
Near Threatened – at risk of becoming threatened soon
Least Concern – not considered at risk
Data Deficient – not enough data to make an assessment
Not Evaluated – not enough evidence or knowledge to assess

Old-growth Gums

Tree-squeak is an old-growth eucalypt tree of which there are more than 700 species! However, to be an 'old-growth' gum, it needs to be at least 170–200 years old and have hollows that animals can nest in. A hollow is produced over time by loss of limbs from wind, lightning strikes, fire, and/or damage caused by termites, other insects, or fungus.

Over 100 species of **vertebrates** rely on these trees and their hollows for their homes. These vertebrates include 81 bird species, 46 mammal species, 31 reptiles, and 16 amphibians, such as frogs. Hundreds more **invertebrate** species such as caterpillars, butterflies, ants, and spiders also rely on these trees.

Glossary

ecosystem – a community of living things that rely on each other to survive

echolocation – the emitting of sound waves and then listening to the echoes that bounce back from objects in their surroundings, which allows bats to navigate and locate prey even in complete darkness

habitat – the natural home or environment of a plant, animal, or other organism

invertebrate – an animal without a backbone

mammal – an animal that gives birth to live young, which suckle on their mother's milk

marsupial – a type of mammal that gives birth to live young, which suckle milk in their mother's pouch

nocturnal – sleeps in the day and is active at night

vertebrates – all animals with a backbone, including mammals, birds, reptiles, amphibians, and fish

"Tree Squeak is a child's delight and may stimulate many a future environmental campaigner. It is based on the truth that our eucalypt trees, the older the better, harbour a galaxy of other living creatures as well as bringing so many other benefits to their greatest threat—we human beings. Robyn O'Neill's Tree Squeak is that best of all literary concoctions—a story which does not thunder but, while offering contentment, also stirs hope for the future. In these beautiful words and illustrations is the promise that Australia's native trees and wildlife will be better respected, better protected, by the next generation."

~ Bob Brown,
environmentalist and former leader of the Australian greens